John Lennon   Jean

IMAGINE

This book is very special to me. The words were written by my husband John and it makes me so happy to see them illustrated in this beautiful book. He wrote Imagine as a song calling for peace around the world. Today, we need peace more than ever, so I think his words are still very important.

Everybody wants to feel happy and to feel safe. And we can all help make the world a better place in our own way. We should always keep love in our hearts, and look after one another. We should always share what we have, and we should stand up for people who are not being treated fairly.

nd it's important that we treat everyone like that, not just our family and our friends. We should treat everybody the same, no matter where they are from or if they speak a different language. After all, the pigeon in this book welcomes all the other birds, whatever colour of feathers or shape of beak they have.

noing this, we can all help to make a difference every day. Every small good thing that w꞉ ꞉ can help change the world for the better. You can do it, I can do it, we all can do it.

Imagine. Together we can make peace happen. Then the world truly will live as one.

— Yoko Ono Lennon

Lincoln

in as   ational UK

No hell below us.

Above us only
sky.

Imagine there's no countries.

It isn't hard to do.

Nothing to kill or die for,

and no religion too.

Imagine all the people
living life in **peace**.

You may say I'm a dreamer,

but I'm not the only one.

I hope some day you'll join us,

and the world will
be as **one**.

Imagine no
possessions.

I wonder if you can.

No need for
greed or hunger.

A **brotherhood**
of man.

Imagine all
the people **sharing**
all the world.

but I'm not the only one.

I **hope** some day
you'll join us,

And the world will
live as one.

Afterword

This book is about peace, which helps us enjoy a happy and safe life. For peace to flourish, we need to treat everyone kindly, equally and fairly.

We also need to look after some precious freedoms called human rights, which protect all of us. Every baby, child and grown-up in the world has human rights. They were first proclaimed in 1948, when the world said 'never again' to the horrors of the Second World War. It was then that the Universal Declaration of Human Rights was born. Human rights are rooted in values such as fairness, truth, equality, love, home and safety. They are part of what make us human and no-one should take them away from us.

Amnesty International works to protect our human rights. We want to say a big thank you to Jean Jullien for his beautiful pictures and to Yoko Ono Lennon for her kindness in letting us use John Lennon's wonderful words in this book.

We want to thank you, too, for helping to make the world a better place.

Thank you.

If you're an adult who enjoys reading with children and you want to explore the values within stories, you can find free downloadable activities for this book and others at www.amnesty.org.uk/education

Amnesty International UK
17-25 New Inn Yard
London EC2A 3EA
Tel 020 7033 1500
sct@amnesty.org.uk
www.amnesty.org.uk

Amnesty International Australia
Locked Bag 23
Broadway
New South Wales 2007
Tel: 1300 300 920
www.amnesty.org.au

Brimming with creative inspiration, how-to projects, and useful information to enrich your everyday life, Quarto Knows is a favourite destination for those pursuing their interests and passions. Visit our site and dig deeper with our books into your area of interest: Quarto Creates, Quarto Cooks, Quarto Homes, Quarto Lives, Quarto Drives, Quarto Explores, Quarto Gifts, or Quarto Kids.

Inspiring | Educating | Creating | Entertaining

First published in the UK in 2017 by Frances Lincoln Children's Books
This paperback edition first published in 2018 in the UK by Lincoln Children's, an imprint of The Quarto Group,
The Old Brewery, 6 Blundell Street London N7 9BH
QuartoKnows.com · Visit our blogs at QuartoKids.com

Important: there are age restrictions for most blogging and social media sites and in many countries parental consent is also required. Always ask permission from your parents. Website information is correct at time of going to press. However, the publishers cannot accept liability for any information or links found on any Internet sites, including third-party websites.

A catalogue record for this book is available from the British Library.

ISBN 978-1-78603-185-3

Published by Rachel Williams · Edited by Jenny Broom
Designed by Nicola Price · Production by Dawn Cameron

Printed in China

9 8 7 6 5 4 3 2 1